WILD AMERICA

SQUIRRELS

By Lee Jacobs

**BLACKBIRCH®
PRESS**

THOMSON

GALE

San Diego • Detroit • New York • San Francisco • Cleveland • New Haven, Conn. • Waterville, Maine • London • Munich

© 2002 by Blackbirch Press™. Blackbirch Press™ is an imprint of The Gale Group, Inc., a division of Thomson Learning, Inc.

Blackbirch Press™ and Thomson Learning™ are trademarks used herein under license.

For more information, contact
The Gale Group, Inc.
27500 Drake Rd.
Farmington Hills, MI 48331-3535
Or you can visit our Internet site at http://www.gale.com

ALL RIGHTS RESERVED
No part of this work covered by the copyright hereon may be reproduced or used in any form or by any means—graphic, electronic, or mechanical, including photocopying, recording, taping, Web distribution or information storage retrieval systems—without the written permission of the publisher.

Every effort has been made to trace the owners of copyrighted material.

Photo Credits: Cover, pages 8, 11 © Digital Stock; back cover, pages 4, 5, 15 © PhotoDisc; pages 3, 6, 8, 9, 10, 14 © Corel Corporation; pages 5, 7, 13, 16, 17, 18–19, 21, 23 © Tom & Pat Leeson Nature Wildlife Photography; pages 7, 12, 22 © Bruce Glassman; pages 16, 19, 20, 22, 23 © Art Today

LIBRARY OF CONGRESS CATALOGING-IN-PUBLICATION DATA

Jacobs, Lee.
  Squirrels / by Lee Jacobs.
     v. cm. — (Wild America)
  Contents: The squirrel's environment — The squirrel body — Social life
— Hunting — The mating game — Squirrels and humans.
  ISBN 1-56711-642-6 (hardback: alk. paper)
  1. Squirrels—Juvenile literature. [1. Squirrels.] I. Title.
  QL737.R68 J33 2003
  599.36—dc21   2002003787

Printed in China
10 9 8 7 6 5 4 3 2 1

Contents

Introduction

Squirrels are rodents and are classified by scientists as members of the order Rodentia. Rodents are mammals that have large, sharp front teeth called incisors. These teeth are used for gnawing. Rodents also have smaller cheek teeth for chewing. Almost half of all species of mammals are rodents.

Within the order Rodentia, squirrels belong to the family Sciuridae. Woodchucks and prairie dogs are also members of this family. Squirrels are everywhere. In fact, there are more than 250 species of squirrels throughout the world. More than 60

Below left: Gray squirrels are among the most common North American species.
Below right: Ground squirrels are most common in areas with few trees.

species live in North America. These species include ground squirrels, such as gophers and chipmunks, red squirrels, and even flying squirrels. The most common squirrels in America are tree squirrels, such as fox squirrels and gray squirrels. (In northern areas, gray squirrels can be black in color and are often mistaken for a different species.)

Flying squirrels live mainly in Asia, but two species are native to North America. They are the northern flying squirrel and the southern flying squirrel. Despite their name, flying squirrels don't really fly. Even though they look like they are flying, they are really gliding from tree to tree. Along each side of its body, a flying squirrel has a long fold of skin called a "patagium." While the creature is sitting still, the flap remains folded. But when the squirrel is ready to glide, it stretches out its arms and legs and leaps from a high tree branch. The folds help it sail from one limb to the next. A flying squirrel can glide a distance of more than 100 feet (30 m)!

Top: Two species of flying squirrels can be found in North America. **Bottom:** Chipmunks are a kind of ground squirrel.

The Squirrel's Environment

Squirrels live in many different habitats throughout North America. They can be found in mountains, deserts, coastal areas, forests, fields, city parks, and neighborhoods around the continent. Squirrels are not very territorial. Each has its own home range where it looks for food and builds its nest. A particular home range, however, is often shared with many other squirrels. Several squirrels may even make nests in the same tree.

Squirrels can be found in nearly every environment.

Common tree squirrels are arboreal. That means they mainly live in trees. These graceful animals run and jump among the trees. They can often be seen and heard leaping from branch to branch, or scurrying up and down tree trunks.

Tree squirrels build their nests high in a tree. A squirrel's nest is called a "drey." It is round in shape and is made from leaves, twigs, grass, and bark. Squirrels sleep and take care of their young in dreys. Squirrels often make more than one drey. And they build thicker dreys in the winter.

Sometimes a tree squirrel will nest in a hole in a tree, or in an abandoned woodpecker hole. Some ground squirrels, such as the 13-lined ground squirrel and the California ground squirrel, build burrows and nest underground.

Tree squirrels will sometimes make their nests inside a tree.
Inset: California ground squirrels dig burrows and nest underground.

Tree squirrels are soft, furry animals with long, bushy tails. A gray squirrel's body is between 8 to 12 inches (20 to 30 cm) in length. Its tail is as long as its body. Fox squirrels are a bit larger, measuring up to 29 inches (74 cm) in combined body and tail length.

Squirrels use their tails for many different purposes. As a squirrel leaps among the trees, its tail can help it navigate—much like the rudder on a sailboat. Squirrels also use their tails to help keep them warm, protect them from the rain, or shade them from the hot sun. (In fact, the squirrel family's scientific name, Sciuridae, means "shade tail" in Greek.) Although ground squirrels are part of the same family as tree squirrels, their tails are not as large and bushy.

Top: Long, bushy tails help squirrels with balance and provide both warmth and shade.
Bottom: Fox squirrels are larger and have longer ears than other squirrels.

8

Squirrels shed their fur twice a year. This is called "molting." Squirrels molt to grow thicker fur coats for the winter and to get rid of their heavy coats in warm weather.

Squirrels have long bodies with strong legs. Their front legs are generally shorter than their back legs. They have sharp claws that help them climb trees and dig for food. The claws also help ground squirrels dig their burrows. A squirrel's front feet each have 4 claws, while the hind (back) feet have 5 claws.

A squirrel's front legs are usually shorter than the back feet. Each front paw has 4 claws.

Squirrels have an excellent sense of smell and good eyesight. Their large eyes are high on their heads, which helps them see in many directions. They also have a well-developed sense of hearing. Tree squirrels generally have bigger eyes and ears than ground squirrels.

A squirrel's sensitive whiskers, or "vibrissae," aid its sense of touch. Squirrels have vibrissae on their faces. They also have them on their legs and feet.

Below left: Large eyes help squirrels to see very well.
Below right: Sensitive whiskers, called vibrissae, help squirrels feel their way around.

Like all rodents, squirrels have front incisor teeth. These teeth grow quickly. Just as people file their fingernails, squirrels keep their incisors worn down by gnawing on hard food, such as seeds and nuts. Squirrels have cheek pouches, where they can store the food they gather. They fill their cheek pouches and then carry their food back to a safe hiding place.

Like all rodents, squirrels have front teeth that grow back as they get worn down.

11

Social Life

Female tree squirrels sometimes live in small groups. They like to huddle together for warmth during cold weather. Ground squirrels—like other ground-dwelling rodents—tend to live in large groups called "colonies." Tree squirrels are active throughout the year. They do not hibernate (sleep through the winter), but they take long rests in their winter dreys. Ground squirrels that live in colder regions do hibernate.

Squirrels have many ways of communicating. Almost all kinds of squirrels rub noses to greet each other. Most types of squirrels can make a lot of noise. They make a

Ground squirrels build large colonies where many families live together.

variety of different sounds to communicate with others of their kind. They grunt, squeal, squawk, chirp, chatter, and even bark at each other. A squirrel that is alone will stay very quiet when predators (animals that hunt other animals for food) are nearby. But a group of squirrels will sometimes join together in a loud chorus of barking to scare off an enemy.

Tree squirrels do not tend to live in large groups.

One type of tree squirrel, called the red squirrel, or chickaree, is very noisy. Chickarees make loud squawking noises at other animals, including people. They may also flick their tails to signal danger. Squirrel predators include owls, hawks, eagles, weasels, wolves, foxes, bobcats, and coyotes. Near human habitats, a pet cat or dog might sometimes catch a squirrel.

Squirrels use their keen senses to stay alert for danger.

Squirrels move quickly and gracefully. Even in the safety of a tree, a squirrel will dart around a tree trunk or hold perfectly still to avoid being seen by an enemy. While on the ground hunting for food—away from the safety of its drey—a squirrel is always on the lookout for predators. It takes a series of short runs when traveling any distance, and stops often to look around for danger. Squirrels can run very fast if a predator is chasing them. Some squirrels can move as fast as 16 miles (25 km) per hour.

Because they have so many natural enemies, squirrels are always on the lookout for predators.

Squirrels are diurnal animals. That means they sleep at night and are active during the day. (Flying squirrels are active at night.) Squirrels begin hunting for food in the morning. Most species are herbivores, which means they mainly eat plants. They gather nuts, seeds, grasses, fruit, and certain kinds of plant buds and blossoms. Some squirrels will also eat insects and bird eggs.

Most squirrels eat a mix of plants, nuts, seeds, fruit, and grasses.

A squirrel will fill its cheek pouches with food before it returns to a hiding place. Ground squirrels often take food back to their burrows. Tree squirrels bury food in different spots. They return to these spots when they are ready to eat.

To hide its food, a squirrel digs a small hole for each nut or acorn. Then it buries the food in the hole and stamps on the dirt to cover it. Squirrels use their excellent sense of smell, not their memory, to help them find their buried supplies. They can find food they have buried up to 12 inches (30 cm) under dirt or snow! To eat, a squirrel sits up on its hind legs and grasps its food with its front paws. Squirrels are expert nutcrackers—they use their incisors to get to the meat inside the shell.

Tree squirrels bury food and return to it another time, when they are ready to eat.

The Mating Game

Most female squirrels are able to have babies by the time they are about 1 year of age. Males are ready to mate at about 18 months. Mating season for many types of squirrels is in the early spring. Several kinds of squirrels mate twice a year, with litters being born in spring and late summer.

Males and females become playful during mating season.

A female squirrel that is ready to mate will often sit in the top of a tall tree and send out a loud mating call. Once male squirrels start to respond to the call, the female starts to move about from tree to tree. The males will chase or follow her. Generally, the female only mates with one of the males.

After successful mating, females are pregnant for between 28 to 45 days. Male tree squirrels do not help raise their young, but male ground squirrels do.

Top: Two squirrels often greet each other by touching noses.
Bottom: Males respond to a female's call during mating season.

Babies

Baby squirrels are called "kittens."
Tree squirrels have smaller litters
of babies than ground squirrels.
A tree squirrel may give birth to 3
or 4 kittens, while a ground squirrel's
litter can be up to 10.

Mother squirrels line their nests
with small tufts of their own belly
fur. This makes the nest soft for the
babies. Kittens are tiny at birth. They
generally weigh less than 1 ounce (28
g) and are only 3 or 4 inches (8 to 10
cm) long. The babies are blind and
have no hair. Kittens need protection
when they are born.

Top right: Kittens are blind and hairless at birth. **Bottom right:** Baby squirrels begin to grow fur at about 3 weeks of age.

If there is danger nearby, a mother squirrel will pick up her babies, one by one, and carry them in her mouth to safety. Mothers nurse their young for about 8 weeks.

By the time they are 3 weeks old, the babies begin to grow fur. About a week later, they open their eyes. After about 6 to 8 weeks, baby squirrels are ready to leave the nest and explore their surroundings. By this time, they have grown fur and look like small adults. The kittens will be full-grown within about 9 months.

A mother squirrel will carry her baby in her mouth if there is danger.

Squirrels and Humans

Humans pose a constant threat to squirrels. Each year, cars kill many thousands of squirrels. In some areas, people hunt squirrels for food or furs. Despite the dangers, squirrels do very well in areas that are heavily populated by humans. Squirrels that live in parks may even become tame enough to let people hand-feed them.

Some people think squirrels are pests. Hungry squirrels, for example, can become nuisances by emptying bird feeders. Filled to the rim with the foods they love, a bird feeder makes an attractive target for squirrels. Bird lovers try many things to keep squirrels out of their bird feeders, but

Left: Squirrels that spend a lot of time around humans become tame.
Below: Some squirrels can be pests.

squirrels usually seem to find a way in. Squirrels can also make a mess by looking through garbage cans for scraps of food or digging up gardens. Squirrels may annoy farmers by eating some of their crops.

Squirrels often damage trees by stripping their bark. If too much of its bark is scratched away, a tree can die. Squirrels can are be extremely helpful to the environment. For example, all of the seed gathering and seed scattering they do helps new trees grow. A tree may grow from a nut or seed that a squirrel has buried and not dug up. And when a squirrel is eating seeds from a pinecone, some will blow away to grow into new pine trees someday.

Squirrels can be trouble, but they can also help the environment. Many scatter seeds and plant acorns or nuts that grow into trees.

Glossary

arboreal living in trees

colony a group of animals or plants of the same kind

diurnal active during the daytime

drey a squirrel's nest

herbivore any animal that feeds mainly on plants

hibernate to sleep through the winter

incisor front teeth with sharp flattened edges

kitten a baby squirrel

molt to shed

patagium fold of skin on a flying squirrel

predator an animal that hunts another animal for food

vibrissae sensitive whiskers of an animal

Further Reading

Books

Bare, Colleen Stanley. *Busy, Busy Squirrels.* New York: Cobblehill Books/Dutton, 1991.

Boring, Mel. *Rabbits, Squirrels and Chipmunks.* Minnetonka, MN: Northword Press, 1996.

Schlein, Miriam. *Squirrel Watching.* New York: HarperCollins Children's Books, 1992.

Web sites

*The Squirrel Almanac—**http://spot.colorado.edu/~halloran/sqrl.html***

Index